Volume 2
1734 to 1783
The Revolution For Freedom

WE HOLD THESE TRUTHS

TO BE SELF-EVIDENT,

THAT ALL MEN ARE CREATED EQUAL,

THAT THEY ARE ENDOWED

BY THEIR CREATOR WITH

CERTAIN INALIENABLE RIGHTS,

THAT AMONG THESE ARE

LIFE, LIBERTY

AND THE PURSUIT OF HAPPINESS.

 PICTORIAL ENCYCLOPEDIA

Volume 2
1734 to 1783
The Revolution For Freedom

Dramatically pictured with new vivid living art and stirring narrative in 16 authoritative volumes to enrich the interest and appreciation of young Americans in their heritage of freedom and equality . . .

Of AMERICAN HISTORY

SPECIAL CONSULTANTS

Bernard S. Miller, ED.D.
Associate Director, John Hay Fellows Program; Collaborator with James B. Conant, *The American High School Today.*

Kenneth W. Lund, PH.D.
Superintendent Oak Park-River Forest High School, Oak Park, Illinois; Chairman, North Central Association Committee on Guidance and Counseling.

Kenneth L. Peters, M.S.
Superintendent of Schools, Beverly Hills Unified School District, Beverly Hills, California.

CONTRIBUTORS

Daniel Powell, M.A.
Teacher, Social Studies Dept., Senn High School, Chicago; John Hay Fellow, University of Chicago.

Commander William M. McCarthy
United States Naval Reserve; Formerly Officer in Charge Press Section Public Information, Navy Department, Washington, D.C.

Pearl J. Slaton, M.A.
Formerly Teacher Public Elementary Schools, McKinley High School, Chicago; Reader, Niles Township High School, Skokie, Illinois.

Earl Schenck Miers
HISTORICAL EXPERT AND AUTHOR.

Jerry Wolfert
HISTORIAN AND AUTHOR.

ILLUSTRATORS and GRAPHIC ARTS
Clarence B. Pontius • Arnold Kohn • Richard Potts • Charles and Esther Spears • Bruce Johnson • Tom Goleas • Michael Balicki • James Axelrod • Lloyd Rognan • Gail Pinchot • Howard Parks • Harry Ekman.

Educational Edition published by
CHILDRENS PRESS, INC. — Chicago

DAVCO PUBLISHING COMPANY • CHICAGO

Forward To Freedom!

ONE hundred and twenty-six years had passed since the first permanent colony was established at Jamestown, Virginia, in 1607. They had been years of peril and hardship—fraught with hunger, privation, plague, intrigue and fear of lurking enemies.

The colonization had ended and the beachhead had been established for future democracy.

The English had founded their thirteen original colonies in America. Last of the thirteen was Georgia, which rose out of the swamplands when James Oglethorpe and thirty-five settlers stepped ashore at Savannah in 1733.

But now all of that was behind the courageous men and women who had left England in quest of new and better homes. Many reasons had impelled them to venture into that new and still mysterious world—reasons which included religious persecution, a domineering government, oppression, poverty and even imprisonment for debts.

What lay ahead, now that the first desperate step had been taken? What did the future hold for the colonists clinging to their seashore footholds from New England to Georgia?

Had they only known! Could they only have foreseen the fight for freedom, the founding of a new nation, and the struggle of that little nation to survive!

The Story of America actually began nearly two-and-a-half centuries before. Christopher Columbus discovered the New World when he sailed from Spain to the West Indies in 1492. John Cabot first reached America sailing for England in 1497. Giovanni Verrazano made France's first official voyage of exploration in 1524.

To those three primary expeditions were anchored the roots of three great colonial empires in America — Spanish, British and French. And out of the roots, through three centuries of strife, grew the thirteen English colonies.

Spain's empire in the south was founded on conquest and the plundering of treasure in Mexico and South America. France's colonization swept over vast northern and central regions in pursuit of hunting and fishing grounds. Along the Atlantic seaboard, the English colonists fought to build homes, cities, and a good life!

The foothold of democracy in America traces back to the first colony in Jamestown. Within twelve years after landing,

the Jamestown settlers won representative government with the House of Burgesses in 1619. One year later, the Pilgrim colony of Plymouth was founded in Massachusetts with the prime purpose of gaining religious freedom. The Pilgrims established self-determination in colonial rule by signing the Mayflower Compact while still aboard ship. The Compact bound the Pilgrims together and established their right to make laws.

Other English colonies followed. After Jamestown and Plymouth came Salem and Boston, where a strong and independent spirit developed from the beginning. Links of the colonial chain were welded together with the addition of Maryland, New York, Pennsylvania, Rhode Island, the Carolinas, and Georgia.

Throughout the 126 years of the colonization, the newcomers from England had found increasing proof that America was the land of which they dreamed.

The seeds were sown for complete religious freedom. Roger Williams proved it when he fled from Puritan domination in Massachusetts and founded Rhode Island at Providence in 1636.

The right of self-government was so deeply rooted that the colonists were willing to fight for it. Nathaniel Bacon proved this when he led a rebellion against oppressive British rule in Virginia in 1676. Jamestown was burned during the rebellion, to keep it out of British hands, and the king had reprimanded his own governor for "tyrannical" deeds.

The colonists also learned that nature had richly endowed this new land of their choice. From New England to Georgia, crops grew bountifully. Vegetables and fruits, food for a man's own table, were to be had for the planting of seeds in the soil around his cabin.

Vast timberlands in the North were the harvest of the woodsman's axe. Grain grew plentifully in the middle colonies. Tobacco and cotton flourished in the South. Everywhere, streams provided cool waters and fishing grounds.

Yes, this was the land—America. The thirteen colonies, standing on the Atlantic shores, resolved to hold and to enrich this flourishing land . . . and to resist at all costs any effort to deny them their rights to independence.

LIFE WAS EXCITING AND DIFFERENT

The colonial coastline ranged from the blustery bays of New England to Georgia's warm seashores. The climate and growing seasons varied accordingly. New England had short growing seasons. The soil became progressively more fertile in the South.

Legislatures were elected by the people, but some had limited powers. Rhode Island and Connecticut elected their own governors. Other governors were appointed either by proprietors holding colony charters or by the king.

Religion and state were closely linked in Protestant New England. Much religious freedom was granted in the middle colonies. Many Southerners were closely connected with the Church of England. Maryland and North Carolina had numerous Catholics.

Trades and agriculture provided the means of living for a majority of the colonists. New England specialized in commerce, fishing and trading. The middle colonies exported much food and other products. Farming predominated in the southern colonies.

A wide variety of crops kept the colonies supplied with abundant food. In New England, garden produce thrived. The middle colonies grew much corn. The South produced tobacco and cotton. All colonies raised cattle.

Skilled workers in all trades laid the foundations of American industry. New England had shipbuilders, metalsmiths, carpenters and artisans. Manufacturing developed in the middle colonies. Slavery increased in the South.

New England pioneered in education. The first public school law was passed and the first college was founded in New England. The middle colonies had a system of private schooling. Rich sons in the South were taught at home or sent to schools elsewhere.

The middle class of workers and farmers were the large majority of Americans. Rich merchants of the North and southern plantation owners were the highest social class—indentured servants and slaves the lowest.

INCREASING CRITICISM of British rule in the American colonies brought about a dramatic climax in 1734. John Peter Zenger, owner of the New York *Weekly Journal*, printed sharp criticisms of Governor William Cosby. The governor charged Zenger with libel and making untruthful statements damaging to his character. By English law any form of injurious statement, whether true or not, was libel. Andrew Hamilton, a famed eighty-year-old Philadelphia lawyer, volunteered to defend Zenger without fee. Hamilton made an eloquent and forceful argument when Zenger went to trial. The spirited old lawyer shouted "this is not the cause of just one poor printer, it is the cause of liberty." The jury returned a verdict of "not guilty." A packed courtroom cheered its enthusiasm and the government's prosecution gasped with chagrin. The John Peter Zenger trial and its outcome established a powerful new aid to American liberty—Freedom of the Press.

A GREAT RELIGIOUS AWAKENING

swept America following the apathy and decline that had set in as an aftermath of church controversies. The Great Awakening took the form of a revival movement sparked by fiery and emotional preaching. The movement ran its course from 1734 to 1744 and brought about many new patterns in religion. Jonathan Edwards, the leader in New England, was regarded as a foremost preacher of the Great Awakening. Edwards, son of a Connecticut clergyman and one of Yale's first graduates, was a highly emotional revivalist. Edwards himself was a Congregationalist minister.

Edwards was one of America's foremost authors and speakers on theology. His preachings and writings gained many followers. George Whitefield, a Methodist minister from England, was a magnetic and vigorous revivalist. He sought to bind all sects in a joint emphasis on God and the Bible. Another leader was John Wesley, who moved from England to Georgia in 1735. Gilbert Tennent was a revival leader in the Middle Colonies. Theodorus J. Frelinghuysen was another of the leaders in the Great Awakening.

All of the revivalists preached a new dedication to worship and church beliefs. It involved not just one church, but all Christian churches. Intense religious differences were stirred up throughout America by the Great Awakening. It brought forth two main conflicting groups, the "Old Lights" and the "New Lights." The "Old Lights" supported established practices and opposed emotionalism in preaching. The "New Lights" supported evangelism and introduced new religious issues. The "Old Lights" scorned the "common, unlearned men" of the new group. They fought determinedly to defend the established order. Politics was injected into the controversy. In Connecticut some "New Lights" were jailed on charges of sedition. This was the result of the pleas that the people also "awaken" to problems of government. The religious connections of the candidates figured for several years in the elections in some towns. The Great Awakening strengthened various sects, such as the Baptists, Methodists and Presbyterians. It inspired the founding of a number of new colleges. The new schools began to grow at once. Among them were New Jersey College (now Princeton), Brown, Rutgers and Dartmouth. Fiery Jonathan Edwards accepted the presidency of New Jersey College just prior to his death in 1758.

NEWFOUNDLAND

CAPE BRETON I.
Louisbourg
★

Quebec ●

NEW FRANCE

Ft. Frontenac
★

★ Ft. Le Boeuf

Ft. Duquesne
★

ENGLISH COLONIES

Atlantic Ocean

KING GEORGE'S WAR spread to their own front door and the colonists rallied to resist. England decided to attack Fort Louisbourg, strong French base on Cape Breton Island off Newfoundland. From Fort Louisbourg, the French had long harried English shipping and fishing in Newfoundland waters. French and Indian forces were based there to attack villages in northern New England. The English sent a fleet to New England under Commodore Peter Warren. New England's militia took up arms under Colonel Pepperell of Maine. Governor William Shirley of Massachusetts planned the campaign. The New England soldiers climbed aboard for the voyage.

Louisbourg was reached and Pepperell's men piled into whaleboats and swarmed ashore. They laid siege to Louisbourg. After forty-nine days of being hemmed in and lashed by frontier-type fighting, the French commander surrendered. The militiamen proudly returned home and were deeply disappointed when England returned Louisbourg to France in a later peace treaty. But they had proved the American colonies had raw fighting material with great potential. Governor Shirley, who planned the campaign, was a lawyer. Colonel Pepperell, who commanded it, was a merchant. Most of the soldiers were farmers, tradesmen and fishermen, but they combined into a bristling, potent force of fighting men.

THE COLONISTS TASTED WAR as they fought for England in King George's War, 1744 to 1748. It was a continuation of England's long struggle with France in Europe, including King William's War and Queen Anne's War. The American part in those conflicts had been mere homefront clashes compared to this war.

NEW SPARKS WERE ADDED to the smouldering French-English rivalry. Bitter competition in trading and fishing continued from Newfoundland to the Great Lakes. Quarrels grew over fishing rights off Nova Scotia and Newfoundland. French fur trading on the Great Lakes was reaping good profits and the English sought this trade. The French had Indian allies in Canadian areas and the English were helped by the Iroquois in the Great Lakes region. The French claimed vast territories in this region as a result of the Mississippi River explorations of Joliet and La Salle. Expanding in that direction, they built forts and trading posts. When the French extended their string of forts into the Ohio River valley (as far as the present Allegheny River) a new battleground developed.

As early as the summer of 1752, open warfare between the French and English began to take shape in America. The French already had built a trading post at the Niagara River portage and had sent Celoron de Bienville to expand the Ohio River Valley holdings. In 1752, the French attacked the trading post at Pickawillany and killed its garrison. Forts were erected at the site of present Erie, Pennsylvania, and on French Creek at its junction with the Allegheny River.

Governor Robert Dinwiddie of Virginia also had aspirations in Ohio. As a private citizen, he bought stock in a newly-formed Ohio Company. As governor, Dinwiddie gave the company a grant of 500,000 acres in the Ohio River valley, despite France's claim to the area. When the French built a fort on the upper Allegheny River, the Virginia governor resented it. Then Dinwiddie further learned the French also planned to build a large fort (now Pittsburgh) at the fork of the Ohio. Now the governor raged.

George Washington made his debut as an American figure when Dinwiddie decided to take action. In 1753 Dinwiddie sent the French commander a demand that he withdraw from Ohio. The bearer of the message was Major George Washington, a twenty-one-year-old Virginia surveyor who also was adjutant-general of the Northern division of Virginia militia. Washington was skilled in the ways of the forest. He reached the French commander and presented the Virginia governor's demand. The Frenchman rejected it. Washington, whose order merely was to present the demand, returned to Virginia. The next year (1754) Dinwiddie sent Washington back. This time the young major was given authority to act. Even as a young man, Washington was known as an inspirational type of leader.

WARFARE FLARED like a forest fire through the Ohio River valley in 1754. When George Washington returned to Virginia and reported the French refusal to leave Ohio, Governor Dinwiddie ordered him back. Dinwiddie had sent workers to build a fort for Virginia at the future site of Pittsburgh on the Ohio River. Washington's orders were to lead troops there and to fight if necessary. Washington led 150 Virginia militiamen through the deep woods. On arrival, he found that the French had beaten the English to it. The French forces had driven off Governor Dinwiddie's workers and completed the large fort for themselves.

The French named the fort Duquesne. The French also built several outpost forts not far from the fork where the present Allegheny and Monongahela Rivers merge to form the Ohio River. When Washington advanced toward Fort Duquesne, he was shadowed by the French. Ten of the French were killed in a fight at Great Meadows. French and Indians rushed from Fort Duquesne to avenge the deaths. Washington retreated to a flimsy defense shelter which he named Fort Necessity. On a sweltering day in July, the French attacked and forced Washington to surrender and leave the Ohio country. Washington and his Virginians, clad in the leather suits of frontiersmen, made the long trip back home. They had lost a battle, but George Washington gained helpful knowledge of a new battlefield.

The French had possession of the Ohio valley. They controlled the shortest route from Quebec to the Gulf Coast across Ohio from Lake Erie and down the Ohio and Mississippi rivers. Washington's fight at Great Meadows was only a small skirmish, but it was the first battle of the French and Indian War with England in America. Out of this conflict grew the Seven Years' War in Europe. European powers at first regarded the Indian war as only frontier fighting. But it grew to involve England, France and Spain, with American possessions the prize at stake.

"UNITE OR DIE!" was Benjamin Franklin's stirring cry to the colonies. He published a cartoon showing a snake cut apart. Each piece represented a colony. If the pieces did not unite, the snake (or colonies) would die. Franklin pleaded this eloquently as he drew up the Albany Plan of Union in 1754. Colonial delegates met at Albany, New York, during June and July 1754. Franklin led the Pennsylvania delegation and drafted the Albany Plan of Union. It proposed a Grand Council composed of members chosen by the colonial legislatures to be coordinators.

A president-general, according to the plan, would be appointed by the king. The Grand Council would maintain a colonial army and levy taxes for common defense. Franklin's plan of union was accepted by the Albany conference, but the individual colonies and the king rejected it. Nevertheless, the idea of union was born. Of particular concern to the colonies was the rising threat of the French as New France rapidly expanded southward. Benjamin Franklin became one of America's most famous and beloved men. He ran away from home in Boston as a seventeen-year-old apprentice printer in 1723. Young Franklin arrived in Philadelphia with a few shillings in his pocket, looking for a job. Within six years he was operator of his own newspaper and print shop.

Franklin was author of the wise and witty *Poor Richard's Almanack*. His Pennsylvania *Gazette* became the *Saturday Evening Post*. Franklin's experiment with a kite provided a momentous scientific discovery. With his son aiding him, Franklin flew the kite, with a key attached to its string, during a thunderstorm. He felt a shock from the key and recognized that the lightning was a form of electricity. Franklin also invented the first practical ventilation stove. Franklin's keen mind was busy at work helping to improve the lives of colonists.

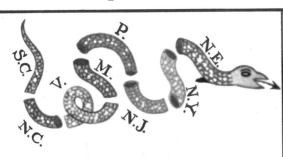

The Albany Plan of Union was advocated by Benjamin Franklin for the mutual protection of the colonies. His cartoon urged them, "Unite or die!"

The Albany Union proposed a grand council, chosen by all the legislatures.

The council head would be a president-general, to be named by king.

A colonial army would be raised, with tax paying cost of defense.

KING GEORGE II HAD ENOUGH of the Ohio Valley failures. He grumbled to his advisors in London, "Conditions are now getting serious in America." In 1755 the king sent General Edward Braddock from England to help the colonists capture Fort Duquesne and drive the French from Ohio. Braddock commanded two smartly-trained regiments of British regulars. George Washington accompanied Braddock in command of Virginia troops. The route to Ohio was difficult and led through the forests. The British soldiers dragged their cannon behind them. On the way, Washington warned the British general that if attacked, his troops should take cover behind trees. Braddock, skilled in European fighting, said it would be a disgrace for British regulars to fight from cover. About eight miles from Fort Duquesne, Braddock's force was attacked from ambush. French and Indians trapped the English in a ravine. The seasoned Virginians took cover. The British regulars huddled in a mass. Here they were easy targets and the French and Indians shot them down from behind trees. General Braddock received a fatal wound. Only the coolness and bravery of George Washington and his capable Virginians averted an even more terrible massacre.

Washington's uniform was riddled by four bullets. Two horses were shot from under him, but Washington led the survivors out of the trap and back to Virginia. The poor leadership of Braddock drew criticism. The British regulars were brave fighters, but did not have a chance. Washington lamented, "We have been beaten, most shamefully beaten, by a handful of men." But Washington emerged as a most expert commander.

STUNNING COMEBACK BLOWS were dealt the French as England made a desperate effort to crush her rival in America. The series of reverses which England suffered previously, helped bring in a new prime minister, William Pitt, in 1758. The aggressive Pitt strengthened the army and chose gifted leaders. New and fresh troops were poured into America. The British navy blocked French shipping off the Canadian coasts. In Pitt's first year, the English captured Fort Duquesne and drove the French out of the Ohio Valley. Duquesne's name was changed to Fort Pitt. Fort Louisbourg on Cape Breton Island was regained. Fort Niagara, Crown Point and Ticonderoga were captured. This left only Quebec and Montreal as major French holdings in North America. An English fleet carrying 9,000 soldiers arrived off the steep cliff at Quebec. General James Wolfe, only thirty-two years old, commanded the British. The powerful fortress of Quebec towered overhead, defended by 16,000 French and Indians under command of Marquis de Montcalm. Wolfe spent two months unsuccessfully trying to blast the French from their stronghold. Then the English discovered a narrow path winding up the steep hillside. Wolfe's men stealthily climbed the path, clinging to roots and jutting rocks.

The next morning Montcalm found the British army gathered on a plateau called the Plains of Abraham, outside Quebec's gates. A bloody battle took place. Both Montcalm and Wolfe were killed. The French were defeated and raised the flag of surrender. Quebec passed into English hands and the next year Montreal surrendered. The backbone of New France was broken by the British.

HIGH-HANDED SEARCH and seizure by British customs officers fanned rebellious fires in the colonies. As the French and Indian War went on, England ordered strict enforcement of writs of assistance. The writs were general search warrants which did not designate a special place to be searched. Any ship, store or home could be entered. Many colonists were engaged in smuggling and trading with France, England's enemy, and the West Indies. They smuggled food to the French and brought back prohibited products. The British customs men invaded the private premises of colonial merchants and seized such property as they pleased. Many colonists were arrested for smuggling and convicted by crown judges on flimsy evidence. Many others found themselves in jail for long periods of time while awaiting their trials. In 1761, the merchants of Boston finally rebelled.

JAMES OTIS ENTERED THE FIGHT when he resigned as advocate-general in Boston to represent the merchants in court. Otis presented a forceful case. He said that random search and long jailing of men without trial violated natural rights. He charged that the colonists' property was being seized illegally. Otis defended the principle that a "man's home is his castle." He said the writs of assistance were an invasion of privacy. He questioned England's wisdom in stretching its authority too far. Otis pointed out that such abuses "cost one king of England his head and another his throne." The court ruled in favor of the crown, but the colonies were greatly impressed. John Adams, Massachusetts patriot, heard Otis and said, "Then and there, the child Independence was born."

Taxation Without Representation is Tyranny

A GREAT CHANGE IN AMERICA resulted when England finally defeated France and Spain. Signing of the Treaty of Paris in 1763 brought vast new territory in America into England's possession. The treaty ended the Seven Years' War in Europe. It also officially ended the French and Indian War in America, although fighting had previously ceased. George III, new king of England, was glad to negotiate with his defeated enemies. England's army and navy had triumphed around the world and won great spoils of war for the nation. France surrendered to England all of Canada and all of her lands east of the Mississippi River except New Orleans. Spain gave England the Spanish Floridas and various islands in the West Indies. France, the major loser, also gave up to Spain, her wartime ally, all French territory west of the Mississippi. Spain retained Cuba and the Philippine Islands. France kept possession of two small islands off Newfoundland to be used as a base for her fishermen. The greatest day of the British Empire had dawned. England's territories in North America were now safe and secure. English sugar plantation owners in the West Indies could expand their trade without fear of competition and attack. For the American colonists it meant new open territories and an easier flow of trade. Warfare with the French in America was forever ended, a great relief to the colonists who had borne arms against the enemy from Canada. But there was one disturbing possibility. Freed of her European strife, England now could turn attention to enforcing a stricter rule on her colonies in America. It was the turning point in relations.

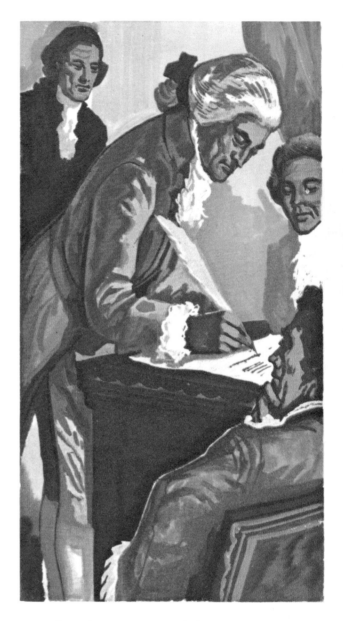

One fear remained for the King of England, too. Presence of a French fighting force in America had kept the colonies on edge. Now with the French threat removed and England's protection no longer needed, a vital restraining shackle had been broken. It gave the American colonies a much freer hand to resist Great Britain's domination as English troops relaxed their hold on the colonies.

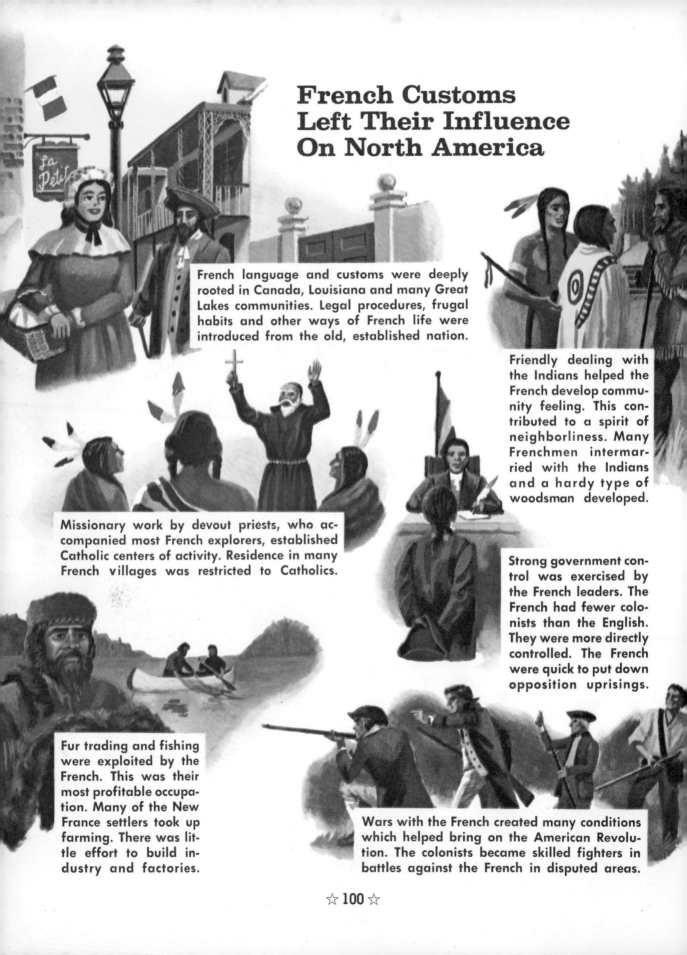

French Customs Left Their Influence On North America

French language and customs were deeply rooted in Canada, Louisiana and many Great Lakes communities. Legal procedures, frugal habits and other ways of French life were introduced from the old, established nation.

Friendly dealing with the Indians helped the French develop community feeling. This contributed to a spirit of neighborliness. Many Frenchmen intermarried with the Indians and a hardy type of woodsman developed.

Missionary work by devout priests, who accompanied most French explorers, established Catholic centers of activity. Residence in many French villages was restricted to Catholics.

Strong government control was exercised by the French leaders. The French had fewer colonists than the English. They were more directly controlled. The French were quick to put down opposition uprisings.

Fur trading and fishing were exploited by the French. This was their most profitable occupation. Many of the New France settlers took up farming. There was little effort to build industry and factories.

Wars with the French created many conditions which helped bring on the American Revolution. The colonists became skilled fighters in battles against the French in disputed areas.

England Drove France From America's Mainland In The French And Indian War

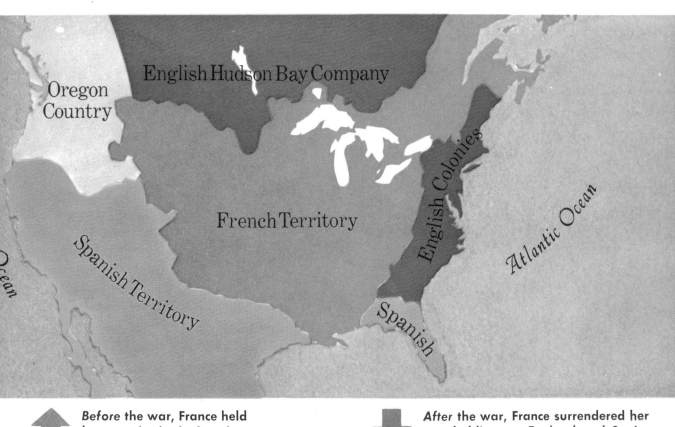

Oregon Country

English Hudson Bay Company

French Territory

English Colonies

Spanish Territory

Atlantic Ocean

Spanish

Ocean

 Before the war, France held large territories in America.

 After the war, France surrendered her vast holdings to England and Spain.

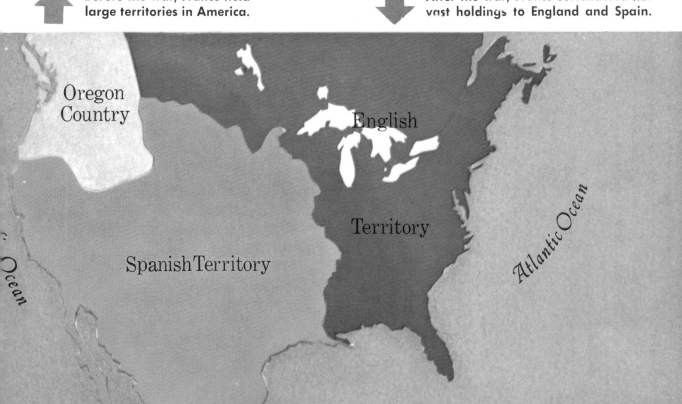

Oregon Country

English

Territory

Spanish Territory

Atlantic Ocean

Ocean

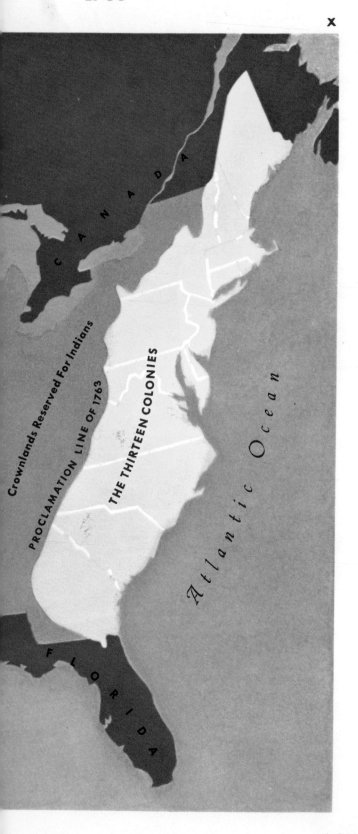

X

A BORDERLINE OF SAFETY was drawn by England in the form of a Proclamation Line. King George III issued the decree in 1763 to discourage pioneers from venturing too far into Indian danger zones. The order was issued five months after Chief Pontiac launched a bloody Ottawa rebellion. It limited the pioneers' advance. The Proclamation Line extended along the crest of the Appalachian Mountains. Territory to the west of the line was put under military rule and settlements in the territory were prohibited.

Another provision opened East and West Florida and Quebec to the migrants. King George hoped this would attract the restless pioneers and divert them from the dangerous Indian lands. But the pioneers chose to ignore the Proclamation Line. They still were lured by the fertile fields of western Pennsylvania and the Ohio River valley. When the fighting with Pontiac died down, the pioneers moved into the region around Fort Pitt. Pontiac finally signed a peace treaty in 1765 and the settlers considered this an opening of the gates. They moved on westward, disdaining the Proclamation Line.

Such strong pressure was exerted by the American colonies that the British were forced to extend the boundary line farther west. This was effected through two treaties negotiated by the English with the Indians. The new line extended the zone of safety into western Virginia and western Pennsylvania. Thousands of settlers hurried into the area, now considered reasonably safe from Indian attack. Many pioneers brought their families. Roads were chopped out of the forests and became heavily traveled. New villages and trade centers had sprung up.

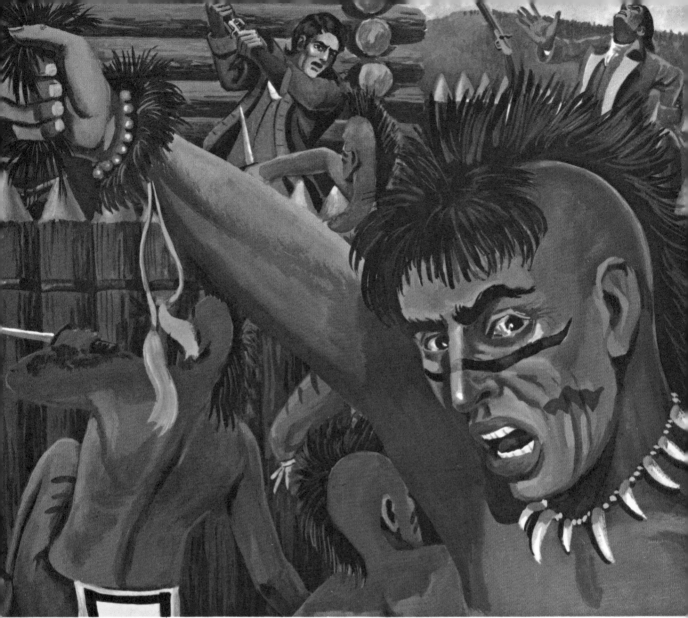

DEATH, FIRE AND SAVAGERY of a far-flung Indian uprising swept the western frontier as pioneers moved into the new English territory. The Indians remained loyal to the French and feared the English would destroy the forests. The French incited the Indians at every opportunity. Pontiac, chief of the Ottawas, plotted an Indian confederacy and most of the territory's tribes joined him. Pontiac's Rebellion had been launched in May, 1763, with an attack on the former French fort at Detroit. Pontiac laid siege when Detroit resisted. The uprising spread across the entire frontier from Niagara to Virginia. All English forts in the West fell except Detroit and Pitt. The garrison at Mackinac was massacred. Hundreds of whites were slain during many months of Indian attacks and burning of villages. Finally, England took forceful action to crush Pontiac's Rebellion. Strong British forces were sent to America. They joined with colonial militia to defeat the Indians near Fort Pitt. Pontiac abandoned his siege at Detroit. The rebellion showed the colonists that westward movement would be stiffly resisted by the Indians.

THE COLONIES FOUND TIME for fun and relaxation in spite of the hardships. There was opportunity for both in the established colonies of the East. Quilting bees, housewarmings, gay tunes by amateur musicians and family celebrations were enjoyed in the homes. Spelling bees and community singing took place in the town halls. Outdoor recreation empha-sized sports. The woods were well stocked with game and the waters with fish. Swimming and boat races, wrestling, running and jumping were favorite athletic tests. People of the Northern colonies enjoyed ice skating and sleigh rides. Fairs offered a variety of games, side shows and horse races. Carnivals were popular in Virginia and other southern colonies.

FRONTIER LIFE WAS DIFFERENT for the pioneers who braved many hazards to migrate to the West. They had gone to make new homes and new lives, and they found themselves in a land beset with peril and hardships. The fear of surprise attack and slaughter by Indians was ever present. Many of the pioneers had only the clothes they wore on their backs and they carried few supplies. They made new clothing from whatever material was available. This often was the pelt of some fur-bearing animal. The pioneers hunted and fished to feed their families. They built rude log cabins with open fireplaces. Wherever they went, the men were armed and ready for a fight with the Indians. They wore powderhorns and knives at their belts. The Indians' French friends had been defeated and driven out and the Indians were bitter against the English. The vast region west of the Alleghenies was under military protection of the British. But only a few troops were stationed there and the colonies gave the British little help in guarding the West. The pioneers were on their own. The newcomers who joined settlements were disappointed to discover that many old French laws still prevailed and there was no representative government. This was one of the conditions the independent pioneers had hoped to avoid by moving. Family life flourished in spite of all the hardships. Couples usually married young, the youths from eighteen to twenty years of age and the girls from fourteen to sixteen. The wedding gifts for the bridegroom might be a horse, a few farming tools and seeds. The bride's dowry often was a cow, a few pieces of furniture and kitchen utensils. Families often were large, the children contributing their share of work to maintain the homes.

There was little opportunity for recreation in the frontier lands. Dances and public entertainment were confined largely to the immediate areas around forts. Such sports as were engaged in consisted of tests of strength and endurance — tree chopping, log rolling, canoe races and target shooting. Family parties took place in closely guarded cabins. Frontier life was vastly different from the comparatively "easy" living the pioneers had left behind them in the colonies back east.

Americans Took Their Place In The World of Culture.

First American artist to win fame was John Singleton Copley (1738-1815) of Boston. He painted Self Portrait. Copley, a sympathizer with British, later made England his home.

Patriotic songs of America were popularized by William Billings (1746-1800). Billings composed many songs which helped stir up patriotic spirit in the American colonies.

Benjamin Franklin founded a magazine on the history of British plantations in America. Although well balanced, the magazine had only a few subscribers.

A pioneer art teacher was Benjamin West (1738-1820). Among his works was the Death of Wolfe. West headed the London Royal Academy.

Thomas Godfrey wrote the first native play, *Prince of Parthia*. First theater was built at Williamsburg in Virginia.

The study of astronomy was pioneered by John Winthrop, Jr., governor of Connecticut. He devised a new system of star study.

Second trade triangle saw the colonists taking grain, meat, lumber and fish to West Indies. Here they picked up products, sent them to England to be sold for cloth and other finished goods.

A BRISK TRIANGULAR TRADE carried on by New England with the West Indies and Africa was threatened in 1764. England adopted a new Sugar Act, which was devised to take a share of the profits. In the Triangular Trade, New England imported molasses from the French and Spanish West Indies. The molasses was manufactured into rum, which was exported to the African coast and exchanged for slaves. The slaves were brought back and traded in the West Indies for molasses. This molasses then was made into more rum in New England and an endless circle of trade was carried on. England's new act actually reduced the duty on molasses from six pennies to three pennies per gallon, but the threat to Triangular Trade was in England's determination to enforce the new duty. The former Molasses Act (1733) was never enforced. The manufacture and trading of rum were important industries in New England. With the new British policy, the smuggling of molasses was increased.

In another three-cornered process, the colonial produce was shipped to Spain and exchanged for wine and fruit. These paid for needed items made in England.

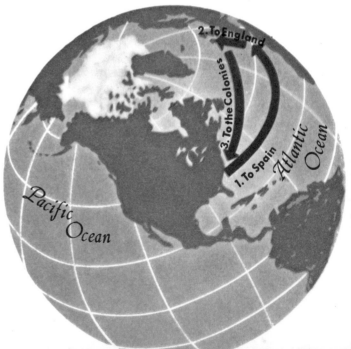

ENGLAND IMPOSED A STAMP ACT on the colonies in February of 1765. The act required revenue stamps on legal documents, newspapers, pamphlets and many types of licenses. The fees ranged from a half-penny to 50 pounds, according to importance of the item. King George III and his minister of finance, George Grenville, adopted the program to bring the colonies under stricter control. England also wanted the colonies to pay their own way in the cost of protecting the western frontier from Indian attacks. Grenville foresaw strong resentment in the colonies. He prepared for it by having Parliament pass a Quartering Act to enforce the new taxes. This act required the colonists to take British troops into their own homes and house and feed them free of cost. The act called for 10,000 troops in America.

Direct taxation by England aroused the most resentment. The Stamp Act marked the first time Parliament itself had voted taxes against the colonies. The Americans had no voice in Parliament and they refused to accept taxation without representation. The most vocal elements, lawyers, publishers and merchants, joined in the chorus of indignation. They pointed out that America was in a post-war depression. They blamed declining incomes on tightening of custom controls and other British restrictive measures.

The House of Burgesses met in May and passed Virginia Resolutions, disputing Parliament's right to tax the colonies. Patrick Henry, a young Virginia lawyer, made a fiery speech before the Burgesses in which he violently attacked King George. The shocked presiding officer of the assembly protested that Henry's speech was treasonable. Henry retorted, "If this be treason, make the most of it!" Other colonial assemblies followed Virginia's lead and passed similar resolutions. Massachusetts invited all colonies to send delegates to a meeting in New York to deliberate a course of action. Nine colonies responded to this invitation.

The Stamp Act Congress was held in October of 1765. Fifty-two delegates represented the nine participating colonies. All delegates had the authority to act. The congress adopted strong resolutions against submitting to taxes leveled directly upon them by England. A report of the colonies' stand was sent to Benjamin Franklin, then in London, with a request that he present these views to Parliament. This marked the first time the colonies took united action against domination by the British Empire.

MOB VIOLENCE BROKE OUT as the people took up the fight against the Stamp Act. The Sons of Liberty and similar clubs were formed. Women organized the Daughters of Liberty. The Sons of Liberty began as an orderly mass protest, but quickly became riotous. Many of the members were unemployed and disgruntled. They blamed loss of their jobs on the depression, which they said had been caused by British taxation. Stormy demonstrations took place throughout the colonies. Property of crown officials was destroyed and lives were threatened. British leaders were hanged in effigy. A mob in Boston plundered the home of Lieutenant-Governor Thomas Hutchinson. The rioters wrecked his furniture and drank his wine. Andrew Oliver, the governor's brother-in-law and a stamp agent in Boston, was dragged under an elm tree and threatened with hanging. Oliver was freed only after swearing he would never sell another stamp. In all colonies, angry crowds destroyed stamp books and manhandled stamp agents. Soon all of the stamp agents resigned.

Colonial merchants boycotted goods from England. Nearly 700,000 pounds in orders were reported canceled, and 4,000,000 pounds in bills unpaid. The merchants in England begged Parliament to aid them as their business dropped so sharply that many faced bankruptcy. At this same time, many liberals in England were sympathetic to the Americans' cause. William Pitt said, "I rejoice that America has resisted," adding "This could make slaves of all Englishmen."

England's merchants joined in the arguments of the home liberals, who were urging repeal of the act. Parliament ignored the colonies' appeal when Franklin presented it, but the other pressure was too great. Yielding to colonial violence and the home merchants' pleas, Parliament repealed the Stamp Act in March of 1766. At the same time, a Declaratory Act was passed, asserting Parliament's right to legislate for the colonies at all times. The colonies were so jubilant over winning the Stamp Act fight they did not immediately recognize the threat carried in the Declaratory Act.

ENGLAND TRIED NEW METHODS of extracting revenue from the colonies in 1767. Charles Townshend, new finance minister, used powers of the Declaratory Act for a series of measures called the Townshend Acts. One act created a Board of Commission of the Customs to enforce the Navigation Acts with writs of assistance. Another act established new duties on glass, paper, painter's supplies and tea. Townshend called them external taxes, meaning that they were to be collected at dockside customs houses. Until then the colonies had not opposed external taxes because these were intended only to regulate trade, and not to provide a means for collecting additional revenue.

This time Townshend proposed to use the tax money to pay the salaries of colonial officials and troops. That made a difference, the colonies argued. The duties were to be used for revenue and, therefore, were ordinary taxes in disguise. The colonies had been paying salaries of the British officials and they feared loss of control if the pay were to come from England. Controversy broke out again. The legislatures of New York and Massachusetts soon were suspended in the dispute.

New riots and violence flared, particularly in New England. Customs agents were mobbed, or tarred and feathered. Colonial merchants once again applied boycott pressure on England. Circulars were distributed reminding the merchants of their earlier nonimportation pledges. Pamphlets urged the people, "Eat nothing, drink nothing, wear nothing that must come from England." English merchants' sales in the American colonies reflected the severity of the boycott and dropped almost one-half as a result.

A SMUGGLING WAR DEVELOPED at Boston as colonial shippers and merchants contrived to evade British application of the new regulations. Smuggling of molasses and other restricted products was widespread and many respected New England businessmen engaged in it. Their ships slipped in and out of Boston harbor at night to avoid duties. Townshend launched a drive to stop them. New customs officials replaced corrupt ones. On July 8, 1768, a colonial ship carrying a cargo of smuggled molasses was seized in Boston harbor by the British. About thirty colonists boarded the vessel late that night and made off with the cargo. John Hancock, a colonial leader and owner of the sloop *Liberty*, was involved in another such incident. The *Liberty* was seized by the British on charges of smuggling wine. The British customs men were elated over catching such a big prize, but their joy was shortlived. A mob of Bostonians boarded the *Liberty*, freed the cargo and severely mistreated the customs officials. Governor Bernard asked the British government to send troops to Boston to protect customs officials and aid in enforcement of the regulations.

British warships anchored in the harbor on September 13. The next morning British soldiers landed and marched into Boston. Jeers from the crowd made it clear the Redcoats were not welcome. The Sons of Liberty decided against further violence at the time. Citizens held a town meeting and warned that the landing and maintaining of a standing army among them was a dangerous infringement of the rights they had enjoyed as colonists.

DANIEL BOONE BLAZED a new trail to the expanding West in 1769 and opened up what is now Kentucky. Boone, a hunter and land surveyor, was sent by Judge Richard Henderson of North Carolina to explore the inviting new territory. With five companions he passed through the Cumberland Mountain Gap on May 1 and entered Kentucky. They were captured by Indians and robbed of their furs and supplies. Boone and his companions escaped and spent the next two winters exploring Kentucky's hills and valleys.

Boone and his men lived off game and fish. For pelts to make jackets and coonskin caps they shot fur-bearing animals. They discovered and explored the lush bluegrass region. Boone dodged Indians and kept constantly on the move. His adventures and resourcefulness made him a renowned woodsman. A great surge of settlers to the West was under way and the frontiers were steadily being pushed back. Land companies helped persuade the government to extend the Proclamation Line. Many Carolinians followed Boone's trail through the Cumberland Gap into the new territory. This route from North Carolina and Southern Virginia became famous as Boone's "Wilderness Road" to Kentucky and Tennessee. The road was a narrow mountain trail through picturesque country. Other Virginians followed the rivers of the region. Pioneers from New Jersey and Pennsylvania forged overland to the Ohio River. They traveled down the broad Ohio on flatboats which were propelled and steered by large oars. It has been estimated that at one time more than 4,000 families were encamped beyond the Allegheny Mountains. They were ready to chop out rough roads and clog them with loaded wagons—all headed for new settlements in "Boone country."

Boone's life was one of continued adventure. He was a blacksmith and teamster during Braddock's campaign in the French and Indian War. Boone established a fort in Kentucky which became Boonesborough. He was a lieutenant colonel in the militia and became sheriff of Fayette County. Boone finally lost his lands and moved to present Missouri.

A DATE LONG REMEMBERED was March 5, 1770. On that day the Boston Massacre took place and Parliament moved to repeal the Townshend Acts. Open friction existed between Boston townsmen and the British. The soldiers were constantly heckled and tavern brawls were frequent. Small boys dogged the Redcoats' footsteps hooting, "Lobsters for sale!" The "massacre" began as a snowball fight. A mob jostled a British sentry at the custom house and eight other Redcoats rushed to his rescue. The crowd pelted them with snowballs and tried to seize a soldier's gun. The weapon was discharged in the struggle and one of the rioters was killed. With no clear order given, the British fired into the crowd. Four more Boston citizens were killed and six were wounded. Thousands of Bostonians walked solemnly behind the hearses at the funeral the next day. For many years the Boston Massacre was commemorated with bitterness. Two American patriots, John Adams and Josiah Quincy, defended the British soldiers in court and claimed self defense. All were acquitted of murder charges. On that same day, March 5, Parliament bowed to English merchants' pleas on the Townshend Acts. The acts were repealed, with a token tax on tea the only measure to be retained. For a time, disorders subsided and there was comparative quiet.

NORTH CAROLINA HAD A WAR of its own in 1771 when the state's western province rebelled against rule by the seaboard section. The westerners considered themselves victims of undemocratic government, corrupt courts, unequal taxation and eastern land speculators. They were rugged farmers and ranchers who had developed the North Carolina back country for themselves. They accused eastern government officials of taking advantage of them. The western towns had vigilante units called "Regulators," who were organized to maintain local order.

The "Regulators" took over their towns' quarrel with the government and many new members joined. A strong contingent of "Regulators" appeared before eastern officials and demanded government changes. The demands included jury trials for debtors, reduction of high court costs, the elimination of tax graft. The West wanted a formal voting law specifying the use of ballots instead of upraised hands. Also demanded were curbs on the eastern land speculators who sought to exploit the territories for the huge profits they were able to realize.

Following the appearance of the "Regulators" Governor Tryon of North Carolina called out the provincial militia to put down the rebellion. After preliminary skirmishes, the two forces met in the "Battle of the Alamance" in May of 1771. A poorly organized army of 2,000 "Regulators" was defeated and the rebellion ended. Some of the "Regulators" were tried for treason and hanged. But most of those who were captured accepted amnesty from Governor Tryon. The "Regulators" were disbanded and many moved with their families to Tennessee.

RHODE ISLANDERS DISLIKED a British revenue cutter named the *Gaspee*. They particularly disliked Lieutenant William Dudingston, the *Gaspee's* commander. Dudingston took delight in his job of capturing smugglers using the Rhode Island coast. He did so with high-handed disregard for the shippers' rights. Dudingston stopped and searched ships at random. He sometimes was accused of thievery when no excuse could be found to confiscate a cargo as contraband. One day the *Gaspee* ran aground on a sandbar off Providence, Rhode Island, The king's cutter was stranded on the sandbar in full view of the Providence townsfolk. They seized upon it as their chance to strike back. On the night of June 9, 1772, dozens of the Providence townsmen swarmed aboard the *Gaspee*. Dudingston and his crew were seized and sent ashore. The hated cutter was burned to the water's edge. A commission appointed to investigate the Gaspee's burning could obtain no concrete evidence. Identities of many of the raiders were common knowledge. One of the leaders of the raid was a prominent merchant, John Brown. But no names were revealed in court or included in the records. The townspeople would not talk. The *Gaspee* investigation ended without action and the British soon dropped the ship's burning as an excuse for reprisal. But the colonies, once they learned the details, did not forget the incident of Dudingston and the *Gaspee*.

Resistance to efforts by England to enforce collection of taxes and duties grew to a blaze beyond the stage of a mere brush fire. Angry citizens of Boston held a mass meeting and demanded withdrawal of the British troops. The British commander moved his soldiers to an island in the harbor. In North Carolina, the governor's troops fired upon a public meeting. Although revolutionary events were moving swiftly, news about them did not. The colonies recognized the need for a system of prompt and effective communications to keep up with conditions.

AN INFORMATION NETWORK was established by colonial leaders to keep each other posted on events in the revolutionary movement. The network was a system of Committees of Correspondence which circulated news of Anglo-American friction. Samuel Adams, Boston's extremist patriot, conceived the idea in 1772. For example, the burning of the *Gaspee* was an exciting instance of colonial resistance. Adams learned that King George III of England planned to pay Massachusetts judges out of customs collected from the colonies. Adams thought this was the type of information which should be made known promptly to each of the colonies.

Adams organized a local Committee of Correspondence in Boston. He had the committee's first letter distributed throughout Massachusetts. Word of the plan spread to patriotic leaders in other colonies and they seized on the idea with enthusiasm. Patrick Henry and Thomas Jefferson led in the formation of a Committee of Correspondence in Virginia. Many members of the House of Burgesses served on the committee. Other colonies also followed the lead of Massachusetts.

All thirteen colonies had Committees of Correspondence in full operation within a short time. The committees circulated reports of every grievance against England and of every act of colonial retaliation. Post riders and fast coastal packets (ships) delivered the reports with special urgency. From New England to Georgia, news now traveled fast. Each report of action strengthened the realization that any loss or gain which affected one colony affected all of the American colonies.

A BITTER CUP OF TEA was brewed for colonial merchants when England passed a Tea Act in 1772. The act was designed to save the British East India Company from bankruptcy. It permitted the company to deliver tea directly to the colonies and sell the tea at company stores. Actually, the colonies now could buy tea more cheaply than they could smuggle it, since English duties were by-passed. But the East India Company's monopoly on local sales shut out the colonial tea merchants. Tea shipments were turned back at New York and Philadelphia because the East India agents feared to accept them. Cargoes were unloaded at Charleston but were stored. Then three tea ships arrived in Boston harbor and when the company agents there insisted on unloading them, Boston arranged a "tea party." On the night of December 16, 1773, fierce whoops rang out along the Boston docks. A war party of about fifty colonists, disguised as Indians, boarded the tea ships, opened 342 chests of tea and dumped the contents in the harbor.

England's Revenge: The Intolerable Acts!

The Port Bill ordered Boston's port closed on June 1, 1774, in reprisal for the Boston Tea Party. Payment was demanded for the tea destroyed by raiders.

Administration of Justice Act provided for trials in England of crown officials accused of major crimes in America. Colonies feared new outrages.

The Massachusetts Government Act gave the governor dictatorial power. Town meetings were limited to fixed dates and only local business could be discussed by townsmen.

A Quartering Act required Massachusetts citizens to take soldiers into their own homes. Also, public buildings could be used for quartering British troops.

The Quebec Act moved boundaries of the province south to the Ohio River and west to the Mississippi. Old French laws were admitted, including curbs on self government.

A CONTINENTAL CONGRESS was called as the colonies' anger rose over Parliament's punishment of Massachusetts and Boston. Leading up to the congress, several colonies passed resolutions condemning the Intolerable Acts. Sympathy was strong for Boston, which was about to be isolated by the closing of its port. Typical was Virginia's dispatch to Boston of thousands of bushels of wheat and corn. The Virginia governor retaliated by dissolving the House of Burgesses. This goaded Virginians into taking the lead in bringing the situation to a head. On May 27, 1774, five days before Boston's port was to be closed, Virginia called on all colonies to hold a continental congress. Committees of Correspondence sprang into action. They spread their letters through the colonies, calling for support of Virginia's proposal.

The Continental Congress was called and opened in Philadelphia on September 5, 1774. Fifty-five delegates represented all colonies except Georgia. The Georgia governor had prohibited an election to name delegates. Outstanding patriot-leaders from other colonies attended, including George Washington, John Adams and Patrick Henry. Extremists, those who advocated vigorous resistance to England, held a slight majority at the congress. The moderates mustered enough strength to block outright war moves, but the extremists were able to force through several aggressive acts.

A Continental Association was formed to choke off British trade with the colonies. British imports were barred after December, 1774, and no more goods were to be sent to England after September, 1775. Another challenge to Parliament was the adoption by the Congress of the Suffolk Resolves, which pledged the colonies not to obey the Intolerable Acts. It was agreed that, unless the grievances were satisfied, a second congress would meet the following May.

Clash Of Interests Erupted Into The Revolutionary War

Domination and taxation without representation in Parliament infuriated the colonies. Loyalty to the king faded as abuses mounted.

Economic interests of colonies and British merchants clashed. The navigation and trade acts cramped colonies' commerce and pinched paper money supply.

Tightened enforcement of colonial laws followed England's defeat of France and Spain. Parliament imposed new taxes and duties.

Forceful leadership inspired a spirit of revolution. Extremists increased anti-British feeling. Colonists showed fighting ability in clashes.

The desire for independence was strengthened by the distance from England. The colonies refused to bow to the British government's remote rule.

Unwise British leadership failed to recognize the colonies' determination to fight for their rights. King George spurned peace bids.

PATRICK HENRY'S ORATORY scorched England again as she retaliated after formation of the Continental Associations. Virginia's Burgesses met in the spring of 1775 to review the situation. Massachusetts had been outlawed by King George III, who declared the colony in open rebellion. The Massachusetts assembly was dissolved but held indignation meetings outside the British lines. General Thomas Gage, the British commander at Boston, was ordered to arrest patriot leaders. Newfoundland waters were closed to Massachusetts fishermen. The colony organized companies of Minutemen, ready to go into action on a minute's notice. They drilled regularly and stocked gun powder and other supplies for quick use.

Virginia took the lead in supporting Massachusetts. The House of Burgesses held a revolutionary convention and Patrick Henry unleashed his oratorical fire. He declared his belief that war with England was inevitable. In ringing tones Henry told the Burgesses, "If we wish to be free, we must fight! I repeat, sir, we must fight! An appeal to arms, and to the God of Hosts, is all that is left to us." Some of the Burgesses had been present ten years before when Henry hurled his memorable defiance of the king, saying "If this be treason, make the most of it!"

Henry goaded those whom he considered timid at the revolutionary convention. He asked, "Shall we resort to entreaty and humble supplication?" In closing his dramatic address, Henry demanded, "Is life so dear, or peace so sweet as to be purchased at the price of chains and slavery? Forbid it, Almighty God! I know not what course others may take, but, as for me, give me liberty or give

me death!" Henry was spokesman for the more ardent Virginia patriots. He was a lanky, sharp-faced country lawyer when he was first elected a Burgessman. Henry won fame in a case which grew out of a Virginia law specifying the manner in which Anglican clergymen were to be paid. The king disallowed the law and several clergymen sued to recover back pay. Henry, opposing them, charged that the British king had "degenerated into a tyrant and forfeited all right to his subjects' obedience." The ministers were awarded only one cent. Patriots carried Henry from the court on their shoulders. Patrick Henry's oratory fired the colonists, welding determination to resist.

"ON TO CONCORD!" General Gage ordered his British troops at Boston. He had instructions to arrest Samuel Adams and John Hancock at Lexington. Gage knew the colonials had powder and arms stored at Concord. He decided to make both seizures at the same time. Sons of Liberty alerted two couriers, Paul Revere and William Dawes. A lantern would be hung in Old North Church when the Redcoats started for Concord. Eight hundred British left Boston late on April 18, 1775. Revere and Dawes saw the lantern signal and rode away to spread the alarm. Revere took the road to Concord while Dawes went to the southwest of Boston. Revere knew the road and the countryside well. He was a rider in the postal service. Revere rode through the night banging on doors and arousing the countryside. "The Redcoats are coming!" Hancock and Adams were awakened at Lexington and fled to safety. The Minutemen at Concord were warned that their supplies were in danger. The Midnight Ride of Paul Revere had accomplished its mission.

A COLONIAL HORNETS' NEST awaited the British on the road to Concord. Dozens of Minutemen, lined up on the village green at Lexington, were told by their commander, "Don't fire unless you are fired on; but if they want a war, it may as well begin here." The Minutemen were fired upon and eight Americans were killed. The British marched on to Concord and met several hundred Minutemen guarding the town bridge. Many Redcoats fell in sharp fighting. Retreating to Boston, the Redcoats' ranks were riddled as Minutemen, townsmen and farmers fired on them all along the way. The British were saved when 1,500 reinforcements sent by Gage joined them near Lexington. On reaching Boston, the British counted 273 of their men killed, wounded or missing. Ninety-three colonists lost their lives as a result of the battle between Americans and crown troops.

THE COLONIALS STRUCK BACK after Concord and seized Fort Ticonderoga on May 10, 1775. All New England was arming for war and ammunition was needed. The British had large stores at Ticonderoga on Lake Champlain. The Connecticut assembly ordered Ethan Allen and Benedict Arnold to capture the fort. Allen, a native of present Vermont, organized a fighting group there known as the Green Mountain Boys. Allen and Arnold led about 230 Green Mountain Boys and militia to the lake shore facing Ticonderoga. Allen and eighty-three of his men rowed across. The landing was at dawn and Allen attacked at once. The Ticonderoga sentries were overpowered and Allen caught the fort's commander dressing in his quarters. Allen swung his sword over the Englishman's head and demanded surrender. "By whose order?" roared the captain. "In the name of the great Jehovah and the Continental Congress!" Allen shouted. The commander surrendered. Many cannon and much powder were found. Two days later the Americans captured Crown Point to the north. They seized more guns and powder. In all, seventy-eight heavy cannon were taken—and two Hudson Valley forts!

A REVOLUTIONARY CRISIS confronted the Second Continental Congress convening at Philadelphia on May 10, 1775. The delegates were grave and deeply troubled men. The colonies were not openly at war with England, but the situation was far out of hand. American blood had been shed and angry patriots were clamoring. The British had marched on Concord and the colonies' own Green Mountain Boys had retaliated by taking Ticonderoga. Colonial leaders were still hopeful of reconciliation, but England had not relented in her attitude and the Americans were determined to stand their ground.

John Hancock of Massachusetts was elected president of the Congress. Every delegate realized the seriousness of the next move. The spirit of the Congress as a whole was revolutionary, but moderates led by John Dickinson of Pennsylvania blocked demands for an immediate declaration of war. But the tide of anger was running strong. Plans were made for tightening up and strengthening the unorganized militia and volunteers milling around Boston. Battle reports from Lexington, Concord and Ticonderoga were analyzed and colonial gains evaluated.

The moderates prevailed and the Congress decided to pursue its efforts to persuade King George III to offer some plan for peace. A letter from England was read, telling how the king persisted in a stubborn attitude. The Revolution was at the crisis point and Congress knew it. Pondering the many problems were distinguished and patriotic men from all of the colonies. Among them was an ardent and talented young lawyer from Virginia, Thomas Jefferson. Also present was the valiant Virginian, George Washington.

GEORGE WASHINGTON was greatly admired by his fellow patriots at the Congress. He was a wealthy plantation owner in Virginia who served with distinction in the House of Burgesses. Washington had proved his military skill and leadership in the French and Indian War. He had shown diplomacy and statesmanship in intercolonial relationships. Associates respected Washington's judgment, decisiveness, and self-sacrifice. Washington was counted on to help secure the South's full participation in case of actual war with England. Washington was born on February 22, 1732, on a Virginia farm called Wakefield. His formal education was cut short. His father died when Washington was sixteen and the son went to work as a surveyor. Years of travel through forests and over rough country gave Washington a rugged physique. He was a major in the Virginia militia at twenty-one. By the time he attended the second Congress, Washington was a polished aristocrat-soldier of forty-three. He was an imposing figure—tall and broad-shouldered, erect and confident. He declared, "I will raise 1,000 men, subsist them at my own expense, and march myself at their head for the relief of Boston."

WASHINGTON WAS CHOSEN by the Continental Congress as commander-in-chief of all colonial troops. On June 15, 1775, Congress raised Washington's rank from colonel to general and unanimously appointed him commander. Congress then adopted the growing but loosely knit militia forces that were gathering to besiege Boston. This was the nucleus of the Continental Army committed to oppose mighty England. A committee for navy, coast guard and marine forces was appointed. Washington modestly did not push for selection as commander-in-chief, although his heart was set on it. Washington's only hint was to wear his uniform while attending sessions of Congress and listening to debate over whether a New Englander should be the military chief. Washington eagerly accepted when the Congress offered him the command. Washington had no military experience by professional standards of Europe, but he was crafty and skilled in the frontier type of fighting. One of Washington's principles was never to let himself be maneuvered into a general engagement. He preferred the strategy of persistently harassing the enemy and disrupting his supply lines, strategy that served effectively throughout the fighting to come.

Shortly after his appointment, Washington left to take command of the colonials at Cambridge. He took a staff of young officers with him. Most of the delegates to Congress still were uncertain about their desire for complete independence from England. King George III and Parliament had declared the colonies to be in open rebellion and had taken drastic steps to suppress them. The Congress decided to make one more effort to restore peace. An appeal was drafted and sent to King George III in an effort to convince him that fighting should be avoided. It was entitled the Olive Branch Petition.

THE BATTLE OF BUNKER HILL was fought before General Washington arrived to take command. The Americans had fortified heights overlooking Boston. On June 17, 1775, the British sent General William Howe with 3,500 troops to take Bunker Hill. The actual battle was fought on nearby Breed's Hill. A force of 1,200 patriots fought under General Putnam, General Warren and Colonel Prescott.

Howe led the Redcoats on their first charge. Waiting until they saw "the whites of their eyes," the colonials opened up with withering fire. The British fled down the hill, leaving many dead. A second charge met the same fate. Howe took the hill on the third attempt as the patriots ran out of ammunition. More than 1,000 British were killed. Colonial losses amounted to approximately 400 soldiers.

A NAVY WAS CREATED by the Continental Congress on October 30, 1775. The Marine Committee was authorized to form the navy and $100,000 was appropriated to fit out armed ships. Esek Hopkins of Rhode Island was named commander-in-chief. Naval regulations were adopted, including a pay scale ranging from $32 a month for captains to $8 a month for seamen. Work began at once on outfitting a few small warships. Seasoned sea captains were selected as commanders and merchant seamen were enlisted as crews. Ex-soldiers picked for combat ability and discipline were formed into a force of Marines. The first American warship was commissioned at Philadelphia in 1776 and a crowd gathered to watch the quarterdeck ceremony. Congress also passed a Prize Law, authorizing private ship owners and their captains to serve as privateers and seize enemy ships. In less than a year, the thirteen American colonies had a naval force at sea. They were now ready to fight wherever there were British.

THOMAS PAINE advocated an outright break with England early in 1776. He wrote a pamphlet called *Common Sense* which was widely read. Paine minced no words in *Common Sense*. He stated flatly that the quarrel with England was beyond peaceful settlement. Paine was an Englishman who had arrived in America only two years earlier. Benjamin Franklin had interested him in the colonial cause. Paine wrote with a simple, direct style that carried force. More than 100,000 copies of Paine's pamphlets were bought.

A tremendous influence on colonial decisions was exerted by Paine's *Common Sense*. Paine hammered at his theme that Parliament, backed by King George III, was denying colonists their rights of life, liberty and property. Paine had been a leader in the group in England which supported the colonies. This group included Edmund Burke, William Pitt and Lord North. Paine, a journalist, decided to emigrate to America and put his convictions in writing. *Common Sense* was the result. Paine despised and often criticized royalty and Parliament. His scorn for the king was expressed with colorful, pointed words when he wrote that "One honest man" was of more value to society than "all the crowned ruffians that ever lived."

Paine fanned colonial resentment by stressing that Parliament ignored all protests and added new abuses. He argued, "To know whether it be the interest of this continent to be independent, we need only ask this easy simple question: Is it the interest of a man to be a boy all his life?" Paine pointed out that blood already had been shed in America. The response to *Common Sense* was immediate and contagious. Indignation of patriots in the American colonies, their sense of justice outraged, neared the boiling point.

George Washington wrote that Paine's pamphlet was "sound doctrine and unanswerable reasoning." As colonial fighting forces swelled, many commanders assembled the troops on drill grounds and had their adjutants read portions of *Common Sense* to them. It was said that Thomas Paine gathered up all the scattered bullets of colonial resistance and welded them into one cannonball. Thomas Paine declared in his daring pamphlet, "The period of debate is closed. Arms as the last resort must decide the contest."

THE BRITISH GAVE UP BOSTON without a fight on March 17, 1776. For six months General Washington had been whipping his colonial troops into shape at Cambridge. He ordered the cannon which had been seized at Ticonderoga brought to Boston. The patriots dragged the heavy artillery by oxcart through forests and over mountains. On arrival of the cannon, Washington gave the British a taste of his strategy by feigning an attack from Cambridge, northwest of Boston. This diverted the attention of General Howe, who had succeeded Gage as the British commander at Boston. Washington and 2,000 men swiftly occupied Dorchester Heights to the south of the city. These heights controlled the road to Boston, but the British had neglected to garrison them. Washington set up his cannon, fortified the heights and demanded withdrawal of the British. The chagrined Howe scoffed at Washington as a "mere militiaman." But he did not choose to risk another setback such as the Battle of Bunker Hill. Howe marched his Redcoats, accompanied by several hundred British sympathizers, to the docks. The group sailed to Halifax in Nova Scotia. Washington and his men moved into Boston, the city remaining in American hands throughout the rest of the war.

THE TIME HAD COME! A definite break for independence was inevitable. The fighting had spread. England was blockading American trade. Some colonies had created their own governments and were seizing British property. On June 7, 1776, Richard Henry Lee of Virginia introduced a resoluton in the Continental Congress for a Declaration of Independence. A committee consisting of Thomas Jefferson, Benjamin Franklin, John Adams, Roger Sherman and Robert R. Livingston was named to draft the declaration. The final draft was largely the work of Jefferson, with a few minor changes by Franklin and Adams. The declaration justified rebellion on the basis of violation of natural rights. It listed grievances against the tyranny of King George III. Members of Congress listened with excitement as the draft of the declaration was read. On July 2, they approved Lee's resolution. On July 4, 1776, the Congress adopted the Declaration of Independence. President Hancock signed it with a flourish—"John Hancock." Benjamin Franklin said, "We must indeed hang together, or most assuredly we shall hang separately." The news touched off jubilant celebrations throughout America. In New York, a lead statue of King George was melted and cast into bullets. The bell in Philadelphia's old State House pealed loudly when the Declaration of Independence was adopted. The State House became famed as Independence Hall and the bell became a symbol of American patriotism as the Liberty Bell.

THOMAS JEFFERSON'S ringing phrases in the Declaration of Independence drove home the theme of freedom. Jefferson was not noted as an orator, but his eloquence flowed from his pen. Jefferson's political thinking had been influenced by the philosophy of John Locke, an analyst of English government. Jefferson adapted long-established English rights to colonial conditions. He combined theory of government with actual experience. He contributed to the Continental Congress a wide variety of talents and a keen mind.

Jefferson was patriot, author, statesman, lawyer, philosopher, scientist and gentleman-farmer. His background was that of a self-made man and he reflected this in his championing of the cause of the people. Jefferson's mother was a member of an aristocratic Virginia family. His father was a pioneer in the frontier region of the colony. When his father died, young Jefferson was left with moderate wealth and heavy family responsibility. Jefferson, born in 1743, spent his youth in Albermarle County. In the same Blue Ridge area, three others destined to greatness, James Madison, Patrick Henry and John Marshall, grew into manhood.

After studying law at William and Mary College, Jefferson was elected to the House of Burgesses. In 1774, Jefferson wrote "A Summary View of the Rights of British America." He noted in 1775 that Virginia's debt to British merchants was 2,000,000 pounds. He pointed out that this was twenty times the amount of money in circulation in Virginia. Thomas Jefferson, then thirty-three years of age, knew exactly what it was he wanted to say when he sat down to write the Declaration of Independence.

MANY COLONISTS remained loyal to England as others fought to gain independence. Early in the Revolution, conflict developed between the Loyalists and the Patriots. The Loyalists, also called Tories, included many from the upper classes, but the majority were in the middle and working classes. John Adams estimated that one-third of the colonists were Loyalists. A large number were concentrated in New York and Pennsylvania. Congress passed a resolution warning against Loyalist activity. The Patriots subjected the Loyalists to much persecution. Mobs seized many suspects and those proved to be Loyalists frequently were tarred and feathered. Some were imprisoned and their property seized. It became common practice for mobs to demand that Loyalist suspects take an oath of allegiance to the Patriot cause. Thousands of the Loyalists fled from the colonies to escape persecution. Many hundreds migrated to Canada, especially to what is now New Brunswick. Some Loyalists moved to England while others departed for the West Indies.

The Loyalists struck back at the Patriots whenever they could. Thousands joined the British troops in America. Some Loyalists even formed their own militia. This occasionally resulted in a pitched battle. On February 27, 1776, a band of Patriots defeated a group of Loyalists at a little crossing called Moore's Creek Bridge in North Carolina. In general, however, the Loyalists lacked vigorous leaders to organize them into a coordinated fighting force. They played no great part in impeding the Revolution.

WASHINGTON LED HIS ARMY from Boston early in the summer of 1776. Uncertain where the British would strike, he moved his headquarters to New York. On June 29, British ships appeared in the harbor. General Howe landed a large army of British regulars and mercenaries on Staten Island. The mercenaries were Hessians, hired soldiers from Germany. The general's brother, Admiral Howe, arrived soon after with reinforcements. British forces now numbered approximately 20,000. Washington, with 10,000 troops, was defeated in a sharp battle on August 27. The Americans were forced back to present Brooklyn Heights, apparently trapped. But Washington slipped across the East River under cover of fog and landed on Manhattan Island. Unable to hold his position, he moved northward to White Plains. Washington recognized the peril his army was facing.

Winter was coming and both manpower and supplies were dwindling. Casualties and expiration of three-month enlistment terms cut Washington's forces greatly. In addition, reinforcements expected from General Charles Lee on the east side of the Hudson River did not reach him. The problem of supply was as acute as that of maintaining fighting strength. There were few production sources and the supply lines were thin and unreliable.

Manpower, food and ammunition became low. Washington decided to retreat across New Jersey into Pennsylvania. That would put the Delaware River between himself and the British. Washington's army marched southward, with the British following closely. The colonials burned bridges and destroyed roads behind them. Washington reached Pennsylvania with only about 3,000 of his men left and a rugged winter ahead.

NATHAN HALE had but one life to give to his country and he proudly gave it. While Washington was still at Manhattan before retreating to Pennsylvania, his position was perilous. He needed to learn British plans before deciding on his own movements, and Hale volunteered to slip behind the British lines. Nathan Hale was a Yale graduate from Connecticut, twenty-one years old. He disguised himself as a school teacher for his perilous mission. He knew that the penalty for being caught spying during wartime was death. The courageous Hale passed the British sentries and obtained valuable information. He was captured by the British while trying to return and report his findings to Washington. Elaborate plans of British forts were found in Hale's boots. The British treated him roughly, and did not even permit him to write one last letter to his family. Hale was hanged on September 22, 1776. As the hangman's noose was placed around his neck the defiant Hale declared, "I only regret I have but one life to lose for my country."

THE FIRST SUBMARINE made its appearance in 1776. It was called the *American Turtle* and was invented by David Bushnell, a young Yale graduate. He wanted to aid the Patriots by sinking British warships. Bushnell had exploded gunpowder under water and that gave him his idea. He built the one-man submarine from oak timber. It had the appearance of a top fashioned from two turtle shells joined together. Vertical and horizontal motion was provided by two propellers, operated by hand from inside the submarine. A "torpedo" was attached to the rudder—a box loaded with gunpowder. Bushnell tried to operate the submarine himself, but he was too frail to manage the craft. Bushnell attempted to surprise and attack British ships in several ports. He was ridiculed when he failed, but he was to become known as the Father of the American Submarine.

WASHINGTON CROSSED the Delaware on December 25, 1776, and delivered a Christmas surprise to the foe. The British had stationed Hessian mercenaries at Trenton to keep watch on the Continental army in Pennsylvania. Washington suspected it would be a night of revelry for the mercenaries and he decided on a surprise attack. It was a stormy night and the Delaware was clogged with cakes of ice as the colonials rowed toward Trenton. A near-blizzard was raging when Washington and his men attacked Trenton early on December 26. The Hessians were at the height of their celebration when the colonials struck. As he had anticipated, Washington caught the enemy surprised and befuddled. In only forty-five minutes of fighting, more than 900 of 1,300 Hessians were killed or captured. Washington seized a large store of supplies and set up an encampment near-

by. The angry British high command at New York sent a force of 6,000 to avenge the Trenton loss. Lord Cornwallis was in command, but he could not catch the crafty Washington. Fires were kept burning in the colonial camp to deceive Cornwallis while Washington and his army slipped away plotting another surprise. On January 3, 1777, the Americans caught the British completely off guard at Princeton, New Jersey, beating them.

Washington moved north to Morristown in New Jersey and set up camp there for the remainder of the winter. The victories at Trenton and Princeton set colonial spirits soaring. Troops who had not understood Washington and thought him over-cautious now regarded him as a great general. Volunteers from all colonies began arriving in increasing numbers. They were drilled throughout the winter at Morristown by hardy veterans.

THE STARS AND STRIPES were first unfurled in the breeze of freedom whipping across America in 1777. Having declared the colonies independent the year before, Congress decided the country needed a flag. On June 14, 1777, the Second Continental Congress adopted the following act: "Resolved that the Flag of the United States be thirteen stripes alternate red and white, that the union be thirteen stars white in a blue field representing a new constellation." This reference was the first official mention of the "United States" as a name for the colonial union. Congress left no records to explain why the colors of red, white and blue were chosen. No definite explanation was given of the flag design. Neither was any official evidence left to support the legend that Betsy Ross, a flag maker of Philadelphia, made the first flag of the United States. Congress decided that there would be only one flag for America. Some nations had one national flag to fly over troops and shore installations, with an ensign for naval vessels. Some also had merchant flags for merchant vessels and battle flags for ground forces. England had a family of flags, each serving a specific purpose. From its creation, America's national emblem was a single all-purpose flag. This was decided upon to symbolize national unity. The new flag waved over troops little more than a year after independence was declared.

DISTINGUISHED VOLUNTEERS from Europe joined George Washington during the summer of 1777. Marquis de Lafayette of France brought with him Baron Johann de Kalb, veteran from Germany. From Poland came Casimir Pulaski and Thaddeus Kosciusko. Baron Friederich von Steuben, expert in technique, came from Prussia. All became key men in Washington's fighting organization and greatly helped the colonial cause. Lafayette figured prominently in the war. DeKalb proved himself a seasoned leader of troops. Pulaski and Kosciusko displayed great fighting ability. Von Steuben contributed his skill as an army engineer. Pulaski and De Kalb lost their lives leading colonial troops in the fight.

Marquis de Lafayette made many sacrifices to join America's fight. The young French nobleman heard a brother of King George III express sympathy for the colonies. Lafayette became fired with the spirit of the Revolution. He bought his own ship and sailed for America with several companions. Lafayette presented to the Continental Congress a letter from a colonial agent in France, recommending that he be commissioned a major general. When the recommendation was ignored, Lafayette then wrote to Congress himself, asking that he be permitted to serve without pay and at his own expense. He also requested permission to serve at first as a volunteer.

Congress was astonished and on July 31, 1777, commissioned Marquis de Lafayette a major general. Baron de Kalb soon was commissioned also. When Lafayette reported to George Washington he was only nineteen years old and his winning ways earned the American general's friendship. Other officers at first resented Lafayette's appointment, but soon they also became his good friends. Lafayette frequently paid the expenses of his own men, spending a great deal of his personal fortune. He was wounded in his very first year of colonial fighting.

Vital help from another source came when Washington needed it most. Two wealthy and patriotic bankers provided funds. They were Haym Salomon of New York and Robert Morris of Philadelphia. Both knew that Washington's troops were ragged, poorly fed and often not paid. They sent their own money and raised all they could from friends. Morris took over the management of Revolutionary War money matters. Salomon spent his entire sizeable fortune aiding the colonies. Their aid proved of great benefit.

THE BRITISH PLANNED a three-pronged pincer movement to cut off New England from the other colonies. General John Burgoyne was ordered to invade from Canada, crossing Lake Champlain and moving toward Albany. Colonel Barry St. Leger was to march eastward from Lake Ontario. General Howe's assignment was to advance up the Hudson River from Manhattan. All three British forces were to meet at Albany and close the pincer. But the plan backfired because the British made blunders and the colonials offered unexpected resistance. Burgoyne sent 1,000 troops into Vermont to seize supplies. Green Mountain Boys under Colonel John Stark waylaid the British and killed or captured 900 of them. St. Leger clashed with backwoods riflemen under General Nicholas Herkimer at Oriskany in the Mohawk Valley. St. Leger's Indian allies deserted and he re-

treated to Canada. Howe completely ignored his part of the British plan. Instead, he chose to move against Philadelphia. Howe landed 17,000 troops at the head of Chesapeake Bay, and Washington rushed to stop him. They met at Brandywine on September 10, 1777, and the far-outnumbered colonials were defeated. At Brandywine, the Stars and Stripes flew for the first time over American troops in regular battle. The Americans lost another fight at Germantown. Howe entered Philadelphia at the end of September. Washington led his seasoned but weary veterans into winter quarters at Valley Forge.

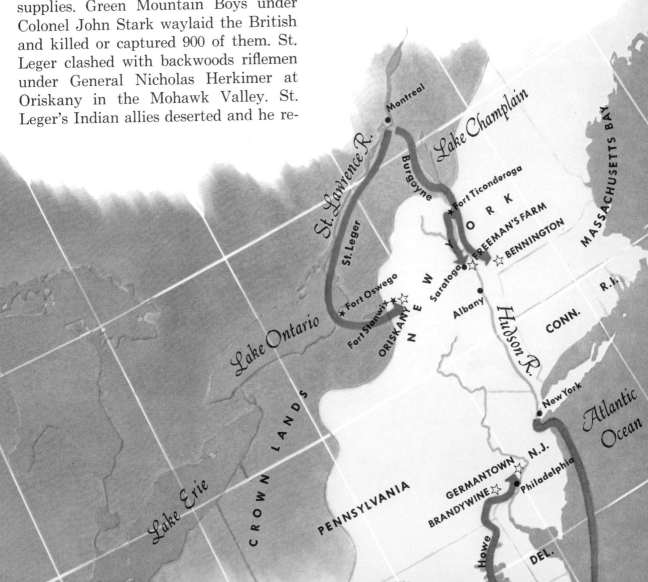

BURGOYNE WAS SURROUNDED and forced to surrender at Saratoga, New York, on October 17, 1777. England's attempted invasion from Canada thus ended in complete collapse. Burgoyne found himself in a critical position after leaving Ticonderoga. The Americans slowed his advance so much that his supplies were exhausted. Battle losses and desertions by Indian allies had cut Burgoyne's original 10,000-man force in half. Wives accompanied some of Burgoyne's officers, bringing along much baggage. Many cannon were left in the forests and supply wagons were wrecked during the march south from Lake Champlain. Meanwhile, new volunteers from New England had joined the colonials. Horatio Gates, the American commander, had 20,000 troops when Burgoyne was surrounded. Burgoyne was said to have been sipping champagne in a parlor when he surrendered. Burgoyne's defeat was a bitter blow for England. Nearly one-third of the British troops in America had been killed or captured. France, hesitant until then, openly negotiated to enter the war on the side of the American colonies.

ARTICLES OF CONFEDERATION were adopted by the Second Continental Congress on November 15, 1777. This was the first national constitution in America. Ratification by all of the states was required before the Confederation could become effective. The colonies finally had agreed upon complete union. The first step was the New England Confederation in 1643. Benjamin Franklin's proposed Albany Plan of Union in 1754 was another step. The Articles of Confederation provided that each state retain its "sovereignty, freedom and independence."

A one-house congress was designed, with the delegates from each state to vote as a unit. No strong executive or national judges were provided for. The Confederation could not pass laws without the approval of nine states. Enforcement was left to the good will of the states. Amendments would need unanimous approval. The new congress would have the power to declare war and make treaties or alliances. It could settle disputes between the various states. The congress had no powers of direct taxation. Money was raised through requisitions on the states. Congress was charged with maintaining postal service and controlling the Indians.

A national citizenship was created. Congress would establish standards of coinage, weights and measures. The Articles of Confederation were sent to the states for ratification. This proceeded slowly as the states wrangled over land claims west of the Appalachians. Seven states had claims in this territory, Virginia's being the largest. As ratification of the Articles of Confederation dragged, the Second Continental Congress continued as the governing body of the land.

A CRUEL WINTER at Valley Forge inflicted a stern test on Washington and his shivering troops. During that winter of 1777-1778, they were encamped on hillsides along the Schuylkill River. They lived in shacks and had little clothing, food or fuel. They faced the full fury of winter's blasts. Washington grieved deeply over the distress of his men. He turned his eyes away as he saw soldiers on guard duty wearing blankets around their shoulders because they had no overcoats. Some recruits shirked duty in their misery, but George Washington refused to punish "men who occupy a cold, bleak hill and sleep under frost and snow."

The killing cold and lack of sanitary facilities further reduced the force. Washington reported that "2,898 men are unfit for duty because they are bare-foot and otherwise naked." Washington frequently used his own money to buy food for the hungry soldiers. Other woes beset Washington during the bleak winter. A plot to replace him as commander-in-chief developed, with several members of Congress taking part. An Irish general named Conway was said to have incited the conspiracy because Washington would not promote him as he had anticipated.

Conway was wounded in a duel with General Cadwallader, a friend of Washington. On his recovery, Conway left America and the plot died. Meanwhile, Howe and his British officers were having a gay time in Philadelphia, only a few miles away. Loyalists entertained them at dinners and balls. Howe had more than 15,000 troops in winter camp at Philadelphia. The British troops were well clothed and well fed. They had comfortable quarters and were in excellent condition. Much dissatisfaction arose in England over Howe's inaction. One critic wrote, "I am of the opinion that any other general in the world than General Howe would have marched on Valley Forge." Howe later was replaced by General Henry Clinton. Thomas Paine, the author of *Common Sense*, commented sadly on Valley Forge's rigors, "These are times that try men's souls." But when the winter was at its worst, colonial hopes came alive with gladsome news from France.

FRANCE CAME INTO THE WAR! The French, long sympathetic, finally became allies of the colonies. Two treaties were signed on February 6, 1778. One pledged friendship and guaranteed France's commercial support. The other treaty bound France and the colonies to fight until American independence was won and both allies were ready to make peace with England. The alliance was gained through Benjamin Franklin's diplomacy. Franklin headed a commission sent to France, with Silas Deane and Arthur Lee as the other members. Comte de Vergennes, the French foreign minister, favored the alliance. King Louis XVI of France hesitated. The colonies' chances of victory were to all appearances remote.

King Louis was reluctant to ally himself with a losing cause against England. Then came the Americans' smashing victory over Burgoyne at Saratoga. Franklin hammered home that now America's chances were bright. He also pointed out that England was making peace overtures. Parliament had offered America every concession short of independence. All taxes and other offensive measures were repealed. The colonies were asked only to acknowledge the rule of the English and the sovereignty of King George.

France was convinced that the situation now held genuine promise. The French hoped to re-establish themselves in America and they saw a chance to help bring England to her knees. France already was giving informal aid, shipping ammunition and supplies to America. Colonial privateers were being fitted out in French ports to prey on English shipping. King Louis was won over and Vergennes was authorized to sign the alliance

treaties bringing France into the fight.

The French-American alliance had an immediate and dramatic effect. The English charged France with interfering in a "family quarrel" and declared war on her old enemy in June, 1778. This took some of the pressure off America as England was forced to disperse her army and navy to defend the British Empire. France provided the colonies increased support with ammunition, supplies, officers, money and naval forces. The French nation was now openly at war with the British. Spain soon decided to join her former ally, France, in this new war against Great Britain. The American colonies spurned the peace overtures from England. The war for independence was far advanced and the colonies were definitely in no mood to abandon it.

THE WAR SWUNG TO THE WEST during the summer of 1778. Several British threats had developed in the area. Massacres at Wyoming Valley in Pennsylvania and Cherry Valley in New York alarmed the entire colonial frontier. Colonel Henry Hamilton, the British commander at Detroit, incited the Indians to raids in what was then called the Illinois country. These raids extended into Kentucky and took a heavy toll. The Kentucky settlements required almost constant protection from fighters stationed in a network of forts. Finally, George Rogers Clark, a young Kentucky surveyor, proposed to Governor Patrick Henry that an end be put to the menace.

Clark suggested a Northwest expedition into the Ohio River Valley and Governor Henry approved. Clark organized several hundred frontier fighters for his campaign. Many of Clark's men were Kentuckians, who were deadly riflemen and skilled Indian fighters. Clark and his men surprised and captured without a fight British forts at Kaskaskia, Cahokia and Vincennes. Hamilton rushed troops to Vincennes, in what is now Indiana, and recaptured it. Later, Clark likewise counterattacked. He and about 175 of his colonial frontiersmen marched 180 miles from Kaskaskia through winter floods and cold. The Wabash and other rivers of the Indiana region were swollen by heavy winter rains and heavier snows.

Clark's men waded through marshes so flooded that the water often reached above their waists. They caught Hamilton's garrison off guard at dusk on February 23, 1779. The British and their Indian allies were enjoying their evening meal when a volley rang out and bullets sprayed the camp. Vincennes surrendered after an all-night fight. Hamilton was taken prisoner and sent to Virginia. Clark took other British forts, and control of the territory north of the Ohio River passed into colonial hands. Settlements in the Kentucky territory were made safe from possible outside attacks.

ACTION WAS STEPPED UP in the South by the British in 1779. They had launched their drive by taking Savannah the year before. Many loyalists in the Carolinas and Georgia went into the British armed service. Others helped by spying on the colonials. But the South also had many fighting patriot leaders, including Francis Marion, Thomas Sumter, Andrew Pickens and "Light Horse Harry" Lee. They waged a guerrilla-type of warfare to harass the British. Typical of these leaders was General Marion who won fame as the "Swamp Fox." The Southern frontiersmen fought as Rangers, independently of the Continental Army. Few had uniforms and food often was scarce. The Rangers kept on the move and Marion's tactics bewildered the British. His men hid in swamps, forests and mountains. They would attack suddenly, crush the enemy, and quickly disappear. Soon they would attack elsewhere, just as unexpectedly. There were isolated actions in various parts of the South during the year. A force of Virginians and North Carolinians led by Colonel Evan Shelby hit Chickamauga Indian villages in Tennessee. Portsmouth and Norfolk, Virginia, were captured and burned by the British forces.

JOHN PAUL JONES won America's first great victory at sea. Although outmatched, he defeated a British opponent in a spectacular battle in 1779. Jones was given his first command in 1775 as the colonial navy was being formed. Jones and his war sloop, the *Ranger*, captured sixteen enemy vessels in three years. Jones then obtained command of five ships outfitted in France. His flagship was the *Bonhomme Richard*, named for Franklin. Off the northeastern coast of England, Jones' little flotilla intercepted a British merchant fleet convoyed by warships. Jones engaged the British flagship, the *Serapis*. The heavier enemy had fortyfour cannon. A thundering battle began on the evening of September 23, 1779, and lasted for three hours. At one point the *Bonhomme Richard* appeared to be sinking. The British commander demanded Jones' surrender. Jones said, "I have not yet begun to fight." He won the day.

BENEDICT ARNOLD turned traitor to the cause he had fought so hard to uphold. Arnold was one of George Washington's most trusted friends. He had served courageously as a general in the American army. Arnold was co-commander in the capture of Ticonderoga. He was second in command when Burgoyne was defeated at Saratoga. He served with distinction at Quebec and in other battles. Then, in 1779, Arnold began more than a year of traitorous dealings with the British. He was military commander of Philadelphia at the time and lavish entertainments ran him into debts which he could not avoid.

Arnold was disgruntled because he had not been promoted. He decided to sell colonial military secrets to the British. Arnold is said to have failed to collect 10,000 pounds promised him in his first arrangement. This temporarily halted negotiations, but Arnold later established a connection with Sir Henry Clinton, the British commanding general. A suspenseful sequence of wartime spying followed. Clinton immediately assigned a young British major, John Andre, to carry on negotiations with the American traitor.

Cleverly masked letters were exchanged between the two. On the surface, they appeared to be correspondence between merchant friends, but there were hidden meanings. Arnold by now had persuaded Washington to transfer him to command at West Point. Arnold agreed through Andre that he would sell to the British drawings of West Point defenses which would enable them to capture the key fort. In exchange, Arnold was to receive a large sum of money and a general's commission in the British army. Andre traveled up the Hudson River to

Haverstraw aboard a small British warship for his meeting with the American.

Arnold and Andre met in a woods and Arnold later delivered the West Point plans at a nearby house. Andre missed connections with his ship and decided to return overland to New York. He changed to civilian attire and that stamped him as a spy. Three loiterers on a road seized Andre. When he offered a large sum of money for his release, the trio became suspicious. They took Andre to the colonial commander at White Plains and the evidence of spying was found on the British agent. On learning this, Arnold escaped to the British warship. Andre was hanged as a spy on October 2, 1780. Arnold served with the British until the end of the war, then remained in England, where he died in poverty. On his deathbed, Arnold is said to have begged to be buried in his old American uniform.

ENGLAND SCHEMED TO WIN the war with its offensive in the South. The plan was to conquer the South and then thrust into the North with a decisive drive. Groundwork for the strategy was laid late in 1778 when the British took Savannah in Georgia. Then, early in 1780, Generals Clinton and Cornwallis landed strong British forces at Charleston, South Carolina. They forced General Benjamin Lincoln to surrender Charleston and 5,000 colonial troops in May. The fighting before and after the surrender was intense.

Bands of Patriots and Loyalists clashed in hand-to-hand skirmishes. Regular troops of both sides rushed in to turn small fights into battles. Nathaniel Greene, the colonial general, reported that South Carolina was "ravaged and plundered by both friends and enemies." After Charleston was overpowered, Clinton returned to New York, leaving Cornwallis in command. The campaign advanced at a leisurely pace and it was August before the British made their next strike. They defeated General Horatio Gates at Camden on August 16, 1780.

Gates' defeat displeased Washington and Greene replaced Gates as colonial commander in the South. The tide of victory temporarily turned. Patriot frontiersmen under Colonel Isaac Shelby killed or captured nearly 1,000 Loyalists and Redcoats at King's Mountain on October 7. General Daniel Morgan defeated the British at Cowpens in January, 1781. Cornwallis and the main British army concluded the southern campaign by winning the Battle of Guilford Court House in March. The victory was costly as Greene's men inflicted heavy losses, but Cornwallis had taken many key points.

THE TABLES WERE TURNED on Cornwallis! The war reached a decision on schedule in 1781, with America and her French allies winning. England was the loser as Cornwallis' plans backfired. On withdrawing from the Carolinas, he walked into a fatal trap in Virginia. Cornwallis marched to Yorktown, located on a peninsula between the York and James Rivers. At his rear was the young Frenchman, Lafayette, commanding Virginia troops. Lafayette closed the neck of the peninsula and a classic of military timing was set in motion. All plans coordinated.

Washington moved south from the Hudson River with American troops. Comte de Rochambeau came down from Newport with a French army. Admiral de Grasse sailed from the West Indies at the head of a French fleet. All converged on Yorktown at the same time! Thundering French guns repulsed a British naval force which sought to enter Chesapeake Bay. Sixteen thousand American and French troops surrounded Yorktown, where Cornwallis had only 8,000 British. With no escape by land and no rescue from the ocean, Cornwallis was trapped.

Yorktown was besieged for seventeen days. The British were under almost continuous fire. French naval guns shelled the town. Washington's and Rochambeau's soldiers stormed over fortifications to capture trenches. The circle around the British tightened. On October 19, 1781, Cornwallis rode out and surrendered to George Washington. His weary and disheartened troops marched away between the American and French lines. The Revolutionary War was not officially over, but the fighting had ended. The Americans had won their independence!

Well–Timed Opportunities Helped The Colonists Win Independence.

Colonial arms were more accurate and were used effectively. Heavy artillery of the British, found useless in forests, often was abandoned.

Forceful leadership inspired a spirit of revolution. Extremists increased anti-British feeling. Colonists showed fighting ability in clashes.

Americans suffered great hardships and privations in their fight for independence. Washington's men survived sternest tests to gain victory.

George Washington was the great leader needed to unify a mixed population and inspire volunteer troops. Washington's tactics outwitted best generals sent by England.

Disagreement in England's government at home and military blunders in America helped the colonies win. The British were forced to employ spiritless mercenaries.

Timely assistance by the French clinched victory. Strong land and sea forces from France joined in the defeat of Cornwallis, ending the fighting with England.

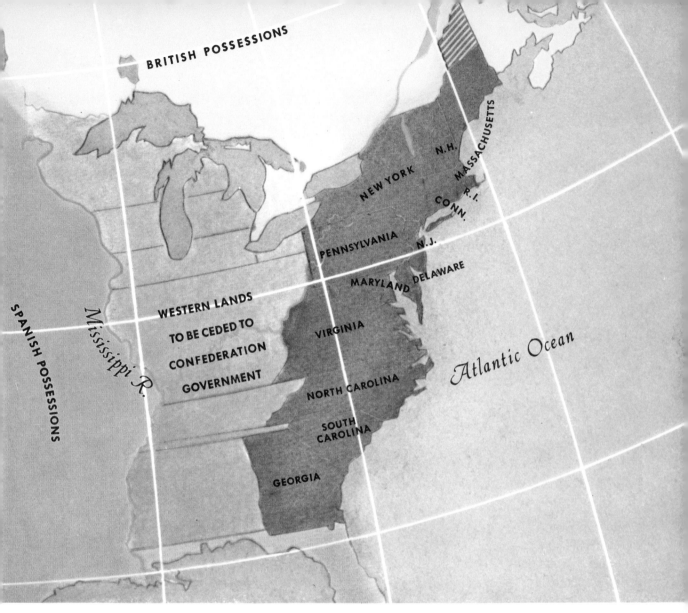

THE ARTICLES OF CONFEDERATION

became effective the same year as the American victory at Yorktown. The Articles of Confederation finally were ratified by Maryland, the last holdout state, in March, 1781. The Articles were adopted by the Second Continental Congress in 1777, but a four-year delay in the necessary ratification by all states was caused by disagreements over land claims. Seven states claimed territory west of the Appalachian Mountains, with Virginia having the largest claims. Several states refused to ratify the Articles of Confed-

eration until the land problem was settled. Maryland, Virginia's neighbor, was the leader in this opposition. It finally was proposed that the states surrender their western lands to the national government. Only Maryland still refused to ratify, but when Virginia agreed to surrender her rights to the land north of the Ohio River, Maryland could delay no longer. She finally ratified the Articles and the Confederation went into effect. Actual surrender of their western lands by all states was not completed for several years after approval of the Articles.

"THE UNITED STATES" was recognized internationally as a name for the American colonies as peace treaty negotiations with England began. Lord Shelburne, prime minister of England, sent Richard Oswald to Paris as his representative. He instructed Oswald, "Treat with the Thirteen United States." Benjamin Franklin headed the commission which negotiated for the United States. John Adams, John Jay and Henry Laurens were the other members. The Americans faced a complication since France was still at war with England and also was allied with Spain. The Americans heard of secret agreements by France and decided that gave them the full right to conclude a separate peace settlement with the English.

Full recognition as a nation was gained by the American colonies. The Paris negotiations began in September, 1782, and a preliminary treaty was signed on November 30. The formal treaty was signed on September 3, 1783. In the Treaty of Paris, the king of England acknowledged the thirteen states to be free and independent. The treaty also established the boundaries of the new American nation. The United States now included all territory between the Appalachian Mountains and the Mississippi River. The northern boundary was Canada (British territory) and the southern limit was Florida (Spanish territory).

American rights to fish in the Gulf of St. Lawrence and off Newfoundland were guaranteed. The United States agreed to ask each state to recognize lawsuits to reclaim property taken from the Loyalists or to collect debts. Franklin's statesmanship won world praise. He first pacified the French. Then he and the commission negotiated favorable terms for the United States. After formal signing of the treaty, the British army sailed home to England. General George Washington led his American soldiers triumphantly into New York on November 25, 1783.

Washington appeared before Congress at Annapolis in December and resigned as commander-in-chief. He refused all offers of pay for his services. He asked only that, when convenient, the young American nation repay him the money he personally had spent to maintain the army. This was estimated at $75,000. At a farewell dinner with his key officers, Washington said with tears in his eyes, "I now take leave of you, most devoutly wishing that your latter days may be as prosperous and happy as your former ones have been glorious and honorable."

America, A New Nation, Begins A New Life

Liberal landholding privileges resulted from a breakdown of aristocracy's monopoly on ownership. Most citizens now could own land if they could buy it.

Freedom of worship was available to all. There were few official churches and individual sects built churches for the use of their individual congregations.

New emphasis on education provided broader opportunities and facilities for more people. America had many new schools and colleges with full courses.

Nature of the population changed as influences of foreign nations diminished. Many Loyalists moved to England after the war. Democracy grew in the young United States.

Frontier lands were open to settlement by those who wanted to establish new homes in the West. But pioneers faced the constant danger of Indian attacks.

Economic changes resulted from the lifting of restrictions on commerce and manufacturing. Free enterprise by firms and individuals was greatly encouraged.

☆ 155 ☆

THE UNITED STATES IN 1783

MASSACHUSETTS
N.H.
R.I.
CONN.
N.J.
DELAWARE
NEW YORK
PENNSYLVANIA
MD.
VIRGINIA
UNITED STATES
NORTH CAROLINA
SOUTH CAROLINA
GEORGIA
Spanish Florida

British Possessions

Missouri R.
Platte
LOUISIANA
Arkansas R.
Canadian R.
Red R.
Mississippi R.
Rio Grande
M E X I C O

Colorado R.

BOUNDARY
NATURAL
Snake R.

OREGON COUNTRY
(Claimed by Russia, Great Britain, Spain
and the United States)

INDEX

TO VOLUME 2

THESE ARE THE TIMES

THAT TRY MEN'S SOULS.

THE SUMMER SOLDIER

AND THE SUNSHINE PATRIOT

WILL, IN THIS CRISIS, SHRINK FROM

THE SERVICE OF THEIR COUNTRY,

BUT HE THAT STANDS IT *NOW*

DESERVES THE LOVE AND THANKS

OF MAN AND WOMAN.

Thomas Paine

Volume 2
1734 to 1783
The Revolution For Freedom